Greetings from
"THE GARDEN CITY OF IOWA"

Greetings from
"THE GARDEN CITY OF IOWA"

Greetings from
"THE GARDEN CITY OF IOWA"

Greetings from
Pella
"THE GARDEN CITY OF IOWA"

Greetings from
"THE GARDEN CITY OF IOWA"

Greetings from
Pella
"THE GARDEN CITY OF IOWA"

Greetings from
Pella
"THE GARDEN CITY OF IOWA"

Greetings from
"THE GARDEN CITY OF IOWA"

Greetings from
"THE GARDEN CITY OF IOWA"

Greetings from
Pella
"THE GARDEN CITY OF IOWA"

Greetings from
"THE GARDEN CITY OF IOWA"

Greetings from
"THE GARDEN CITY OF IOWA"

Greetings from
Pella
"THE GARDEN CITY OF IOWA"

Greetings from
Pella
"THE GARDEN CITY OF IOWA"

Greetings from
"THE GARDEN CITY OF IOWA"

Greetings from
Pella
"THE GARDEN CITY OF IOWA"

Greetings from
Pella
"THE GARDEN CITY OF IOWA"

Greetings from
Pella
"THE GARDEN CITY OF IOWA"

Greetings from
Pella
"THE GARDEN CITY OF IOWA"

Greetings from
"THE GARDEN CITY OF IOWA"

Greetings from
Pella
"THE GARDEN CITY OF IOWA"

Greetings from
"THE GARDEN CITY OF IOWA"

Greetings from
Pella
"THE GARDEN CITY OF IOWA"

Greetings from
Pella
"THE GARDEN CITY OF IOWA"

Greetings from
"THE GARDEN CITY OF IOWA"

Greetings from
"THE GARDEN CITY OF IOWA"

Greetings from
Pella
"THE GARDEN CITY OF IOWA"

Greetings from
Pella
"THE GARDEN CITY OF IOWA"

Greetings from
"THE GARDEN CITY OF IOWA"

Greetings from
"THE GARDEN CITY OF IOWA"

Greetings from
Pella
"THE GARDEN CITY OF IOWA"

Greetings from
"THE GARDEN CITY OF IOWA"

Greetings from
Pella
"THE GARDEN CITY OF IOWA"

Greetings from
"THE GARDEN CITY OF IOWA"

Greetings from
"THE GARDEN CITY OF IOWA"

Greetings from
"THE GARDEN CITY OF IOWA"

Greetings from
Pella
"THE GARDEN CITY OF IOWA"

Greetings from
"THE GARDEN CITY OF IOWA"

Greetings from
"THE GARDEN CITY OF IOWA"

Greetings from
"THE GARDEN CITY OF IOWA"

Greetings from
Pella
"THE GARDEN CITY OF IOWA"

Greetings from
"THE GARDEN CITY OF IOWA"

Greetings from
Pella
"THE GARDEN CITY OF IOWA"

Greetings from
THE GARDEN CITY OF IOWA

Greetings from
"THE GARDEN CITY OF IOWA"

Greetings from
"THE GARDEN CITY OF IOWA"

Greetings from
Pella
"THE GARDEN CITY OF IOWA"

Greetings from
"THE GARDEN CITY OF IOWA"

Greetings from
"THE GARDEN CITY OF IOWA"

Greetings from
Pella
"THE GARDEN CITY OF IOWA"

Greetings from
"THE GARDEN CITY OF IOWA"

Greetings from
"THE GARDEN CITY OF IOWA"

Greetings from
"THE GARDEN CITY OF IOWA"

Greetings from
"THE GARDEN CITY OF IOWA"

Greetings from
Pella
"THE GARDEN CITY OF IOWA"

Greetings from
Pella
"THE GARDEN CITY OF IOWA"

Greetings from
"THE GARDEN CITY OF IOWA"

Greetings from
"THE GARDEN CITY OF IOWA"

Greetings from
"THE GARDEN CITY OF IOWA"

Greetings from
"THE GARDEN CITY OF IOWA"

Greetings from
Pella
"THE GARDEN CITY OF IOWA"

Greetings from
Pella
"THE GARDEN CITY OF IOWA"

Greetings from
Pella
"THE GARDEN CITY OF IOWA"

Greetings from
"THE GARDEN CITY OF IOWA"

Greetings from
"THE GARDEN CITY OF IOWA"

Greetings from
"THE GARDEN CITY OF IOWA"

Greetings from
"THE GARDEN CITY OF IOWA"

Greetings from
Pella
"THE GARDEN CITY OF IOWA"

Greetings from
"THE GARDEN CITY OF IOWA"

Greetings from
Pella
"THE GARDEN CITY OF IOWA"

Greetings from
THE GARDEN CITY OF IOWA

Greetings from
"THE GARDEN CITY OF IOWA"

Greetings from
"THE GARDEN CITY OF IOWA"

Greetings from
Pella
"THE GARDEN CITY OF IOWA"

Greetings from
"THE GARDEN CITY OF IOWA"

Printed in the USA
CPSIA information can be obtained
at www.ICGtesting.com
CBHW021555300624
10899CB00013B/323

9 798385 413584